www.providencebooks.net

Publisher Contact

Email:contact@providencebooks.net

Social media: facebook.com/providencebooks

Acknowledgements

The team at Providence Books would like to thank our friends, family, suppliers and customers for making our vision of creating the highest-quality books a reality. Thanks for purchasing and enjoy the quotes!

This page is intentionally left blank

This page is intentionally left blank

A lot of people simply don't realize their potential because they're just so risk adverse. They just don't want to take the risk.

Benjamin Carson

And I've always said, 'If two people think the same thing about everything, one of them isn't necessary.' We need to be able to understand that if we're going to make real progress.

Benjamin Carson

Before this country came on the scene, for thousands of years people did things the same way. Within 200 years of the advent of this nation, men were walking on the moon, and I want us to recognize this is the kind of people that we are. We're creative with a lot of ingenuity and a lot of energy.

Benjamin Carson

But, you know, we have these entrenched entities - and I'm talking about both Republicans and Democrats - who believe that when you're elected to office, you become some kind of member of the aristocracy, and that anyone who challenges you is attacking you and is unpatriotic. This is foolishness.

Benjamin Carson

Corporations are not in business to be social-welfare organizations; they are there to make money.

Benjamin Carson

Don't let anyone turn you into a slave. You're a slave if you let the media tell you that sports and entertainment are more important than developing your brain.

Benjamin Carson

Economics is not brain surgery.

Benjamin Carson

Education is a fundamental principle of what made America a success. We can't afford to throw any young people away.

Benjamin Carson

Even if you're Bill Gates, you've got problems. I'm sure he would probably easily give a few billion dollars to get rid of all the problems that he has.

Benjamin Carson

Every person is endowed with God-given abilities, and we must cultivate every ounce of talent we have in order to maintain our pinnacle position in the world.

Benjamin Carson

Every time I am looking into the depths of somebody's brain, I'm thinking, 'This is what makes a person who they are. That structure contains memories. Everything that they've ever experienced is right in there.'

Benjamin Carson

Evolution and creationism both require faith. It's just a matter of where you choose to place that faith.

Benjamin Carson

God has opened many doors of opportunity throughout my lifetime, but I believe the greatest of those doors was allowing me to be born in the United States of America.

Benjamin Carson

Health care is one-sixth of our economy. If the government can control that, they can control just about everything. We need to understand what is going on, because there are much more economic models that can be used to give us good health care than what we have now.

Benjamin Carson

Here's a nation, one of the founding pillars was freedom of speech and freedom of expression. And yet, we have imposed upon people restrictions on what they can say, on what they can think. And the media is the largest proponent of this, crucifying people who say things really quite innocently.

Benjamin Carson

I actually don't think that I'm that much smarter than anybody else. It's just that I frequently just seem to know what to do, and I think that's wisdom.

Benjamin Carson

I always pray for God's guidance in my life and he always provides it. He opens the right doors he shuts the right doors. And I have tremendous faith in him. He just guided my career in an amazing way.

Benjamin Carson

I believe that things are always going to work out, even if in the beginning it doesn't look like they are working out. I know in the long run they are going to work out, and it's going to be fine.

Benjamin Carson

I could easily have decided that life was cruel, that being black meant everything was stacked against me.

Benjamin Carson

I detest politics, to be honest with you. It's a cesspool. And I don't think I would fare well in that cesspool because I don't believe in political correctness and I certainly don't believe in dishonesty.

Benjamin Carson

I don't want my kids to grow up with no father like I did. I came to the conclusion a while ago that you can work until midnight and not be finished or you can work until 6 or 7 and not be finished. I decided I'd rather work until 6 or 7.

Benjamin Carson

I first wanted to be a psychiatrist. I decided against that in medical school when I discovered that psychiatrists didn't, in reality, do what they did on TV.

Benjamin Carson

I have no problem whatsoever with allowing gay people to live as they please, as long as they don't try to impose their lifestyle on everyone else.

Benjamin Carson

I have this feeling that as time goes on, we're not getting any more civilized, and we should be. We're still running around like the days of Genghis Khan. There are so many important, better things to do and we need to encourage people to reach into the brighter side of humanity and not encourage people to continue to glorify the darker side.

Benjamin Carson

I pray before I go into the operating room for every case, and I ask him to give me wisdom, to help me to know what to do - and not only for operating, but for everything.

Benjamin Carson

I serve God, and my purpose is to please Him, and if God be for you, who can be against you?

Benjamin Carson

I started reading about people of great accomplishment... and it dawned on me suddenly that the person who has the most to do with what happens in your life is you.

Benjamin Carson

I think one of the keys to leadership is recognizing that everybody has gifts and talents. A good leader will learn how to harness those gifts toward the same goal.

Benjamin Carson

I want the government to provide the military so we don't get invaded by somebody and destroyed. I want the government to provide the roads so I can get from point A to B. In terms of taking care of my day to day needs, I want to do that myself. I want my community to do that.

Benjamin Carson

I was definitely an at-risk kid growing up.

Benjamin Carson

I was perhaps the worst student you have ever seen. You know, I thought I was stupid, all my classmates thought I was stupid, so there was general agreement.

Benjamin Carson

I would like people to recognize in looking at my story that the person who has the most to do with what happens to you is you. It's not the environment, it's not the other people who were there trying to help you or trying to stop you. It's what you decide to do and how much effort you put behind it.

Benjamin Carson

I would never turn my back on my fellow citizens.

Benjamin Carson

I would prefer to just continue to speak about truth and to speak about what makes sense.

Benjamin Carson

I've had experiences in my life that leave no doubt in my mind about the fact that God exists. I'm quite willing to debate people who don't think so because I want them to explain to me how did our solar system get so organized and how is the universe so complex and yet well-organized that we can predict 70 years hence when a comet is coming?

Benjamin Carson

If God thinks proportionality is fair who are we to say that it is unfair?

Benjamin Carson

If we can take young people who excel at the highest levels, put them on the same kind of pedestal as the all-state basketball player and the all-state football player, and begin to get the same kind of recognition, it will have a profound effect, and we are finding that it does.

Benjamin Carson

If you go and talk to most people, they mean well but they don't have much of a breadth on education, of knowledge of understanding what the real issues are and therefore they listen to pundits on television who tell them what they are supposed to think and they keep repeating that until pretty soon they say, 'Oh, well that must be true.'

Benjamin Carson

Illogical thinkers throw names and slurs around because they have no arguments with which to rebut their opponents. Rational people have to keep hammering their points home.

Benjamin Carson

In general I was a good kid. It usually took a lot to make me mad. But once I reached the boiling point, I lost all rational control. Totally without thinking, when my anger was aroused, I grabbed the nearest brick, rock, or stick to bash someone. It was as if I had no conscious will in the matter.

Benjamin Carson

In my own personal life, God plays a great role in the risk, because I pray before I go into the operating room for every case, and I ask him to give me wisdom, to help me to know what to do - and not only for operating, but for everything.

Benjamin Carson

Intelligent people tend to talk about the facts. They don't sit around and call each other names. That's what you can find on a third grade playground.

Benjamin Carson

It doesn't matter if you come from the inner city. People who fail in life are people who find lots of excuses. It's never too late for a person to recognize that they have potential in themselves.

Benjamin Carson

It's very important for people to know themselves and understand what their value system is, because if you don't know what your value system is, then you don't know what risks are worth taking and which ones are worth avoiding.

Benjamin Carson

Kids have what I call a built-in hypocrisy antenna that comes up and blocks out what you're saying when you're being a hypocrite.

Benjamin Carson

Let's let everybody believe what they want to believe. And that means, P.C. police, don't you be coming down on people who believe in God and who believe in Jesus.

Benjamin Carson

Marriage is a very sacred institution and should not be degraded by allowing every other type of relationship to be made equivalent to it.

Benjamin Carson

My favorite subject was recess. Fortunately for me, I had a mother who believed I was smart.

Benjamin Carson

My strong belief is that God created human beings and therefore he knows about every aspect of the human body. So if I want to fix it, I just need to stay in harmony with Him.

Benjamin Carson

My thoughts are that marriage is between a man and a woman.

Benjamin Carson

No matter how good you are at planning, the pressure never goes away. So I don't fight it. I feed off it. I turn pressure into motivation to do my best.

Benjamin Carson

Nobody is starving on the streets. We've always taken care of them. We take care of our own; we always have. It is not the government's responsibility.

Benjamin Carson

One of the reasons surgeons have so much trouble separating Siamese twins is that nobody gets to do many of them. On the table, the anatomy is so different from normal, that you're constantly trying to figure out, 'Can I cut this? Does this wire lead to what?' It's like trying to defuse a bomb.

Benjamin Carson

Our children need to see and hear about more black role models in many fields so they can make better choices.

Benjamin Carson

Our schools too often want to shut people up so they can't talk about real solutions. People who think differently tend to clam up because they think something is wrong with their ideas.

Benjamin Carson

Over the years my mother's steadfast faith in God has inspired me, particularly when I had to perform extremely difficult surgical procedures or when I found myself faced with my own medical scare.

Benjamin Carson

People all over the nation are starved for honesty and common sense.

Benjamin Carson

People spending more of their own money on routine health care would make the system more competitive and transparent and restore the confidence between the patients and the doctors without government rationing.

Benjamin Carson

Quite frankly, having an uninformed populace works extremely well, particularly when you have a media that doesn't understand its responsibility and feels more like it's an arm of a political party. They can really take advantage of an uninformed populace.

Benjamin Carson

Resist this war on God, freedom of religion and freedom of speech.

Benjamin Carson

So after a while, if people won't accept your excuses, you stop looking for them.

Benjamin Carson

The P.C. police are out in force at all times... We've reached a point where people are actually afraid to talk about what they want to say.

Benjamin Carson

The Roman Empire was very, very much like us. They lost their moral core, their sense of values in terms of who they were. And after all of those things converged together, they just went right down the tubes very quickly.

Benjamin Carson

The key is to cut out the middleman and empower both doctor and patient with information about what things cost.

Benjamin Carson

The mind controls so much of the body. We are much more than flesh and blood; we are complex systems. Patients do better when they have faith that they're going to do better. That's why I always tell my patients and their families not to neglect their prayers. There's nobody I don't say that to.

Benjamin Carson

The most important thing for me is having a relationship with God. To know that the owner, the creator of the universe loves you, sent His Son to die for your sins; that's very empowering. Knowing Him and knowing that He loves me gives me encouragement and confidence to move forward.

Benjamin Carson

There are a group of people who would like to silence everybody and have everybody go along to get along, but that's not going to be very helpful for us in the long run, in terms of solving our problems. And somebody has to be courageous enough to actually stand up to, you know, the bullies.

Benjamin Carson

There is a tendency of people to try to make you believe only a few people are smart. As a brain surgeon, I know better than that.

Benjamin Carson

There is no fulfillment in things whatsoever. And I think one of the reasons that depression reigns supreme amongst the rich and famous is some of them thought that maybe those things would bring them happiness. But what, in fact, does is having a cause, having a passion. And that's really what gives life's true meaning.

Benjamin Carson

There is no job more important than parenting. This I believe.

Benjamin Carson

There is no one that we can afford to throw away.

Benjamin Carson

There is so much potential out there in young people and they aren't getting the right information or being encouraged in the right ways. This is our duty as a society.

Benjamin Carson

There's a certain spiritual nature and something of the mind that we can't measure. We can't find it. With all our sophisticated equipment, we cannot monitor or define it, and yet it's there.

Benjamin Carson

There's absolutely no reason at all that physicians, scientists, shouldn't be involved in things that affect all of us.

Benjamin Carson

There's no question that as science, knowledge and technology advance, that we will attempt to do more significant things. And there's no question that we will always have to temper those things with ethics.

Benjamin Carson

This is a country for, of, and by the people not for, of, and by the government. If we turn it over to them we cannot complain about what they're doing because this is a natural course of men and we have to hold their feet to the fire.

Benjamin Carson

Those of us who believe in God and derive our sense of right and wrong and ethics from God's Word really have no difficulty whatsoever defining where our ethics come from. People who believe in survival of the fittest might have more difficulty deriving where their ethics come from. A lot of evolutionists are very ethical people.

Benjamin Carson

Through hard work, perseverance and a faith in God, you can live your dreams.

Benjamin Carson

We are more than just flesh and bones. There's a certain spiritual nature and something of the mind that we can't measure. We can't find it. With all our sophisticated equipment, we cannot monitor or define it, and yet it's there.

Benjamin Carson

We have much more in common with other people than we have apart.

Benjamin Carson

We live in a country that used to have a can-do attitude, and now we have a 'what-can-you-do-for-me?' attitude, and what I try to do is find ways that we can develop common ground.

Benjamin Carson

We need to find ways to elevate the expectations, particularly of those individuals who may start off on a lower socioeconomic rung, who might be seen as disadvantaged. But, you know, the reason I say be seen as disadvantaged, it's because life is so short, and there's so much that can change.

Benjamin Carson

We need to understand that we are not each others' enemies in this country. And it is only the political class that derives its power by creating friction. It is only the media that derives its importance by creating friction... that uses every little thing to create this chasm between people. This is not who we are.

Benjamin Carson

We should be concerned not only about the health of individual patients, but also the health of our entire society.

Benjamin Carson

We're not planning for the future. If we continue to spend ourselves into oblivion, we are going to destroy this nation.

Benjamin Carson

Well, I say that the most important job you can possibly have is raising a child, and it needs to be treated that way. You have to show them, rather than just talk to them.

Benjamin Carson

Well, when did this become a monarchy? You know, we are the people. The president works for us and, you know, we need to remember that.

Benjamin Carson

What do lawyers learn in law school? They learn to win...
What we've got to start thinking about is how do we solve
problems.

Benjamin Carson

What we need to do in this PC world is forget about unanimity
of speech and unanimity of thought and we need to concentrate
on being respectful of those people with whom we disagree.

Benjamin Carson

What you're saying is that 'I, the superior elite, will take care of
you.' Why? Because, you see, that superior, elite group needs
to feel superior and elite. And they can't be superior and elite
unless you have a whole lot of people down there groveling
around. So you keep them down there by feeding them.

Benjamin Carson

When I entered high school I was an A-student, but not for
long. I wanted the fancy clothes. I wanted to hang out with the
guys. I went from being an A-student to a B-student to a C-
student, but I didn't care. I was getting the high fives and the
low fives and the pats on the back. I was cool.

Benjamin Carson

When I look at the human brain I'm still in awe of it.

Benjamin Carson

With everything that is complex, we learn. If you don't learn, then it's an utter and abject failure. If you do learn, and you're able to apply that to the next situation, then you take away a measure of success.

Benjamin Carson

You can understand why I'm a believer. I have seen miracles.

Benjamin Carson

You can't allow the forces of political correction to shut you up. I mean, why are people afraid to say, 'Merry Christmas?' Give me a break. If people don't like it, yeah, they can go do something else.

Benjamin Carson

You don't have to be a brain surgeon to be a valuable person. You become valuable because of the knowledge that you have. And that doesn't mean you won't fail sometimes. The important thing is to keep trying.

Benjamin Carson

You have the ability to choose which way you want to go. You have to believe great things are going to happen in your life. Do everything you can - prepare, pray and achieve - to make it happen.

Benjamin Carson

You know, I'm a physician. I like to diagnose things. And, you know, I've diagnosed some pretty, pretty significant issues that I think a lot of people resonate with.

Benjamin Carson

You know, many people have said that I'm on the edge and I'm maverick for some of the big operations that I've done. I'm not at all. I pray; I ask God to give me wisdom, 'Should I do it?', guidance in terms of how to do it, who to consult with. All those kind of things are incredibly important.

Benjamin Carson

You need an incredible amount of self-confidence to go digging around in someone's brain.

Benjamin Carson

You're going to be much less likely to point the finger at somebody and create a huge brouhaha when it wasn't necessary if you had stopped and asked yourself, 'Could I have done things to prevent this situation?'

Benjamin Carson

This page is intentionally left blank

This page is intentionally left blank

This page is intentionally left blank

This page is intentionally left blank

This page is intentionally left blank